VANISHING CULTURES

SAHARA

JAN REYNOLDS

LEE & LOW BOOKS INC. • NEW YORK

To my father, Smith Seeley,

and all loving fathers around the world—J.R.

Manufactured in China by Jade Productions, December 2016

Photographic work supported by the Professional Photography Division of Eastman Kodak Co.

Original design by Camilla Filancia
Lee & Low Edition design by Rich Deas
Book production by The Kids at Our House

The text is set in Palatino

1 2 3 4 5 6 7 8 9 10 (HC)   (PB) 10 9 8 7 6
First Lee & Low Books Inc. Edition, 2007

Library of Congress Cataloging-in-Publication Data
Reynolds, Jan.
Sahara : vanishing cultures / by Jan Reynolds. — 1st Lee & Low Books ed.
p. cm.
Originally published: San Diego : Harcourt Brace Jovanovich, ©1991.
Summary:"Describes the way of life of the Tuaregs, a nomadic culture that presently exists in the Sahara,
the world's largest desert"—Provided by publisher.
ISBN-13: 978-1-60060-146-0 (hardcover)   ISBN-13: 978-1-60060-131-6 (paperback)
1. Tuaregs—Juvenile literature. 2. Sahara—Social life and customs—Juvenile literature. I. Title.
DT346.T7R66 2007

305.89'33—dc22   2006029267

MIX
Paper from
responsible sources
FSC
www.fsc.org   FSC® C111080

The Tuareg live in the middle of a dry, hot land called the Sahara, the largest desert on earth. They make simple, portable homes out of dried grasses and camel leather so they can easily travel from place to place to find water. Because they move so often, they are called nomads, and when they travel with their camels carrying the few items they own, they are called a caravan. Sometimes the Tuareg make long journeys called trade caravans, traveling great distances across the desert to exchange such items as salt and dates with other people for items they need but cannot find in the Sahara.

But this ancient way of life is disappearing. Airplanes and trucks crossing the Sahara have taken the place of the old trade routes and camel caravans across the desert.

Although the Tuareg may appear different from us because of the way they spend their days, we all share the same feelings and basic needs. We really are all alike no matter where we live. We all belong to the same family, the human family, and every time a culture disappears, we lose a part of ourselves. Because of this, perhaps we should take a look at life in the Sahara before it vanishes forever.

As the sun drops behind the Hoggar Mountains in the center of the Sahara, the largest desert on earth, a young boy named Manda asks his father to tell him a story about their tribe, the Tuareg.

Evening breezes sweep across the hot sands, cooling the desert. Manda creeps closer to the fire, and his father begins his tale.

"Long ago, Tuareg men rode proudly on their camels. They covered their faces with cloth veils so only their eyes could be seen, making them look fierce and noble. They were called the Blue Men because the dark blue dye in their robes would rub off on their skin. The Tuareg rode camels in caravans, carrying wonderful things like ostrich feathers, salt, parrots, and even ivory and gold."

In the warm glow of the fire, Manda soon falls asleep.

Early the next morning, while Manda is still asleep, his mother sifts a grain called *couscous* to remove small pebbles from it before making the breakfast porridge. Manda's little brother gathers the family's goats together so his mother can milk them after breakfast. But one little goat slips away to climb a tree and nibble on the thorny branches.

Manda's mother milking the goats

After breakfast, Manda helps his father. He holds a camel while his father removes the hobbles — pieces of rope or leather that tie a camel's legs together.

Camels are hobbled so they cannot go too far away as they search for food. But sometimes they do wander off, and then Manda's father must find them. He can spend half a day looking for them, following their footprints in the hot sand.

While Manda helps his father, his little brother stays cool in a shade tree, watching a neighbor woman use clay to turn camel hide into leather. She makes bags and tents out of this strong, tough leather.

Manda's mother crushes sweet, dried dates for everyone in the village to eat. She uses a large bowl to hold the dates and crushes them with a heavy piece of wood.

Soon Manda's little brother visits the old woman who lives by the village garden. She cuts the end off a dried gourd so he can use it as a ball to play with.

He also stops by the deep well to say hello to some friends who are getting water for their families.

Although the desert is very hot and dry, there is water. After a hard rain, it collects along narrow washes. Hardy grasses and flowers grow in these areas.

The Tuareg know they will be able to find water flowing underground all year long in such places. With water they can grow beautiful gardens in the desert.

Manda's little brother plays in the village garden, measuring himself against the tall wheat. Even though the sun is going down, it is still very hot, but in the garden the air feels a little cooler.

The next day, while Manda and his little brother are letting the goats out and looking for their camels, their mother is making thin pancakes for breakfast. She cooks them over an open fire inside their hut.

And outside, their father is making a sweet, mint tea called *atai*, the favorite drink of the Tuareg.

After breakfast, Manda's father says he will need Manda's help. They are going to caravan their camels to the races at the camel festival. Once the camels are ready to go, Manda can't help smiling with pride as he leads the caravan away from the village.

Manda's caravan

Outside the village, Manda's father helps him climb into the saddle. Manda holds tight while the camel rocks back and forth as it stands up.

Riding close behind his father, Manda guides his camel around the small bushes and large rocks of the desert. At midday, they stop to rest and eat. Manda is given the honor of carefully taking the saddle off his own camel.

Manda's father makes tea, and in the hot sand underneath the fire he cooks bread to eat.

This is an important time for Manda. When the caravan reaches the site of the races, he will wear a veil for the first time. But his head must be carefully shaved so the veil will fit just right. When the caravan begins again, Manda sits proudly in the saddle, this time leading the caravan just like a desert trader of long ago.

As evening approaches, Manda and his father stop at a friend's camp. Instead of grass huts, these Tuareg live in camelskin tents with walls made of woven grass.

Nearby are large rock carvings made by people who lived in the desert long before Manda and his family.

The next morning, Manda's father fills his water bag, which is made from the skin of a goat. The caravan still has a long journey ahead, far across the desert sands.

Manda's father in his best robes

When they finally reach the site of the festival, Manda's father puts on his best robes and veil. Following tradition, Manda darkens the skin around his eyes and brow with ashes before putting on his own veil.

Soon the riders gather. The camels are dressed in their finest saddles, handwoven blankets, and decorations.

The riders walk their camels slowly out over the hot sands. Then, suddenly, one man turns and shouts. The race is on. With their robes waving in the wind, the riders urge their camels to run faster and faster.

But, surprisingly, no one really cares who wins. For the Tuareg, it is the way a man rides his camel that is important. The style of the camel rider is the Tuareg's most valued art.

It is the camel dance after the race that is the most important event of the festival. The men show off their skills for the group of women they circle on their camels.

In the evening, Manda gathers his camels to rest for the night. Manda loves living in the desert, and he is proud to be one of the Tuareg with his own camel caravan.

I traveled to the edge of the Hoggar Mountains, which rise ten thousand feet in the center of the Sahara. A friend I had made in the village where I was staying introduced me to Alitni, Manda's father, when he rode in one day with his camels. All I could see of Alitni, dressed in his flowing robes and dark veil, were his eyes. He was tall and walked in a regal, stately way. This man was one of the last nomadic camel breeders of the Sahara. His look burned through me, sizing me up to see if I might be fit enough for hard travel on camelback for several days through the desert. As we rode off into the scorching sun, I had to laugh at how comfortable I felt with someone I had never met before, whose face I couldn't even see, and with whom I could only converse through hand gestures. I would be alone with Alitni for days, totally dependent in a foreign, hostile environment.

The Tuareg are called the Blue Men of the desert. Water is scarce, so precious indigo dye is beaten, instead of boiled, into their clothing, and it rubs off on their skin. Consequently, blue skin is a status symbol; the darker the shade of blue you are, the wealthier you appear. The shiny, metallic-blue veil Alitni wore was a real curiosity to me. I had heard many different tales explaining why the men covered their faces so completely, but my favorite was: "Why do I wear the veil? Because I am one of the Tuareg!"

Alitni and I rode together in the soft silence of the desert. A consistent breeze several feet off the ground made the ride pleasant in the dry heat. Our camels walked with a loping, lulling gait that I found very soothing. These amazing beasts can withstand the torrid, barren territory by storing fat in their humps and water in their bloodstream and stomachs. But not being a camel myself, I wondered where we would find water. The three and a half million square miles of the Sahara, an area slightly larger than the mainland U.S., averages less than five inches of rainfall per year, but there are occasional downpours that create gullies of water several feet deep. Even years later, these washes often have water running beneath them, so we traveled the washes Alitni knew. He would occasionally dismount and dig down a couple of feet to uncover water for us. It was always brown and gritty, but satisfying nonetheless. We also carried water in goatskin bags that, when full, looked like goats with their heads lopped off.

The nights were beautiful. Under a sky full of brilliant stars, we lay by the small fire that baked our bread and boiled our sweet, mint tea. Life was simple. I felt I could truly understand the Tuareg saying: "To wander is to be free. To live permanently is to be shackled."

In a few days we reached the encampment—a handful of dried-grass huts clustered on the edge of a wash. The women came to greet Alitni and were surprised to see me. The Tuareg society is matriarchal; the lineage follows the women because "it's the belly that holds the child." The women wear no veils, and they are the ones who are better educated, who teach the children, and who create the oral histories and poems the Tuareg are known for. After many days at the encampment, word spread that the celebration of the camel races would be occurring soon—the moon would be full. Alitni decided it was time he took his son Manda on caravan to learn how to manage the camels. Pride ran deep in Manda's heart, although his face appeared shy and unsure as his camel took lead of the caravan, and we rode away from camp. Manda was alert, looking here and there, questioning his father as we rode.

The Tuareg are experts in desert navigation—finding wells demands tremendous skill. Whole caravans can vanish when calculations are off by a mere fraction. Some believe the Tuareg choose their course across the sands by celestial navigation, but it seems more likely their keen eye for intimate details of their surroundings helps them steer their course. The major trade route for the Tuareg was across the Sahara to Tripoli, the gateway of Africa. They carried such things as gold, ivory, ostrich feathers, pepper, kola nuts, and live parrots, and they returned with goods like cloth, rugs, and metals. The Tuareg also ran caravans to the south for trading salt. Pillaging of caravans was not uncommon in the Sahara, and perhaps raiding was necessary for the most resourceful tribes to survive in this harsh environment.

Across the horizon we spotted two camel trains drawing near. When our paths eventually crossed, the men adjusted their veils to cover their mouths—it is a sign of disrespect to show your mouth to a stranger. Alitni greeted each man as if he were speaking to two people because the Tuareg believe everyone has a spiritual guide who is always with them. It was decided we should all join together for the last day of our journey to the festival. At dawn the day we would reach the festival, I saw something I never expected—the men were applying ashes to their eyelashes and brows before wrapping their twenty-foot veils around their heads. (I was so surprised that when I jumped up to photograph Manda applying this makeup, I accidentally shot my pink tennis shoes in the background.) It wasn't long before we rode into the midst of a fantasia of color, sound, and smell. Thousands had gathered for the two-day celebration. Huts and tents sprang up everywhere, like flowers after a sudden rain.

Amidst all the excitement, in the dust and heat, the race took place. The riders came charging into the throng of people, and to my surprise the winner was not discernible and was quite unimportant. These men were more concerned with their appearance in their finest robes and running their handsome camels to show off their skills as riders. Their goal was to give an artful display of their fearlessness, as they rode together in an aggressive band. In fact, the main purpose of the event is to impress the women, who literally cannot see the men under the veils and robes, so they choose their suitors by the way the men ride the camels. After the race, the riders quickly encircled a large group of women who were clapping and singing to them, and they began to trot their camels round and round. This ceremony, called the *Ilugan,* displays the elegance and sublimity of the rider.

The smell of fresh baked earth stirred up into the dry air, dust muting the setting sun, and the sound of the drumbeats in rhythm with the animals' hooves, blending with the high voices singing an almost forgotten melody, gave me an intimate sense of what it means to be part of the Tuareg culture—a people proud of their way of life, their animals, and their land.

—*Jan Reynolds*